# Medical Technology
## AND ENGINEERING

DYS DYS DYS DYS DYS DYS DYS DYS DYS DYS DY
85b 388 389I 389II 390 391 392 393 426 438 439 44
17 16 13 15 19 14 17 16 13 15 19

By Carla Mooney

www.rourkeeducationalmedia.com

PHOTO CREDITS:
Front Cover: © Henrik Jonsson, alengo, jpa1999, Jacom Stephens, Ashok Rodrigues, Mark Kostich, mikeuk, Woodooart; Title page: © Pgiam; Table of contents © Nicolas Loran; Page 4 © DNY59, Steve Jacobs; Page 5 © Eric hood, Ivan Burmistrov; Page 6-7 © melhi, Mlenny Photography; Page 8 © Classix, Eric Hood, Miodrag Gajic; Page 9 © Laurin Rinder, Aleksandar Jocic; Page 10 © Sebastian Kaulitzki, Jaco Wolmarans, bojan fatur; Page 11 © Alexander Oshvintsev; Page 12 © Stephen Coburn, luismmolina; Page 13 © Christopher Futcher, Jacom Stephens; Page 14 © Andres Rodriguez, itsmejust, Hanhanpeggy; Page 15 © kali9, Arturo M. Enriquez, yumiyum, BanksPhotos; Page 16 © Ciprian Florin Dumitrescu, Robyn Mackenzie, Cammeraydave, Charles Nieuwenboom, Ruslan Dashinsky; Page 17 © Aprescindere, Mark Herreid, Vesna Njagulj, Luis Carlos Torres, Levent Konuk; Page 18 © Alexei Averianov, Iakov Filimonov, Stratum, Ingwio; Page 19 © kali9, BanksPhotos; Page 20 © FotografiaBasica, Stígur Karlsson; Page 21 © Dmitry Mordvintsev, Sergey Chushkin, Neustockimages, Ryan Balderas, uchar; Page 22 © Showface; Page 23 © atbaei; Page 24 © Yunxiang987, Sean Locke, Chris Bernard, Nancy Nehring; Page 25 © Cosmin - Constantin Sava, Olha Rohulya, DNY59; Page 26 © Ingrid Prats, Niko Guido; Page 27 © jamesbenet, SisterSarah, mediaphotos, Roman Sigaev; Page 28 © Andrei Malov, aaM Photography, Ltd.; Page 29 © Paul Vinten, Juanmonino; Page 30 © Norman Chan, Katseyephoto, Jan Rihak, Piotr Wzietek; Page 31 © Dmitry Berkut, Dr. Heinz Linke; Page 32 © Michael Miller; Page 33 © hakan dogu, David Kevitch; Page 34 © MichaelSvoboda; Page 35 © Leah-Anne Thompson, Medical Art Inc; Page 36 © ranplett, fansshare.com, Vladislav Gajic; Page 37 © MichaelSvoboda, wikipedia. org, Warenemy; Page 38 © David Gunn, CoryDavisImages; Page 39 © ASSOCIATED PRESS, GENE J. PUSKAR; Page 40 © mark wragg; Page 41 © sgame, Nicolas Loran, Shunyu Fan; Page 42 © Iqoncept, Evgeny Terentev, Pgiam; Page 43 © dra_schwartz, Dmitry Knorre; Page 44 © Oksana Pasishnychenko, Glazyuk; Page 45 © Andrey Armyagov

Edited by Precious McKenzie

Cover design & interior layout by Cory Davis

**Library of Congress PCN Data**

Medical Technology and Engineering / Carla Mooney
(Let's Explore Science)
ISBN 978-1-61810-123-5 (hard cover) (alk. paper)
ISBN 978-1-61810-256-0 (soft cover)
Library of Congress Control Number: 2011945268

Rourke Educational Media
Printed in the United States of America,
North Mankato, Minnesota

**Also Available as:**

Educational Media

rourkeeducationalmedia.com

customerservice@rourkeeducationalmedia.com • PO Box 643328 Vero Beach, Florida 32964

# Table of Contents

# CHAPTER ONE
# what is medical technology?

Today, doctors use many tools to help people feel better. **Antibiotics** fight infections. Blood tests **diagnose** disease. An artificial leg helps a person walk. All of these are examples of medical technology. Medical technology is the use of science to solve heath problems.

Before medical technology, the world was very different. Imagine living with no medical tests, machines, or medicine. Disease was a mystery. People did not know why they became sick. They did not have tools and medicines to help them feel better. Many people died from infections and illnesses.

**Antibiotics**

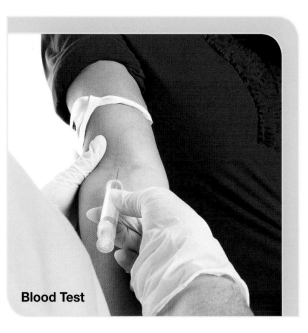

**Blood Test**

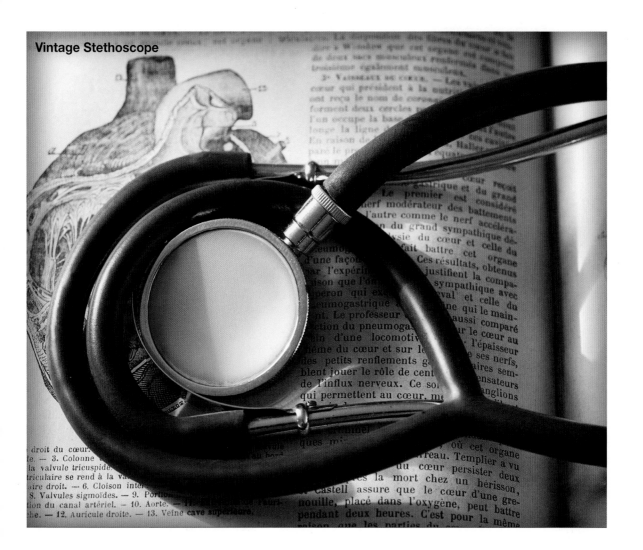

**Vintage Stethoscope**

Before the 19th century, doctors could not see or hear inside a living body. After the patient died, doctors could cut open the body and look inside it. Yet this did not help doctors diagnose or treat illness in living patients. Some of the earliest breakthroughs in medical technology allowed doctors to see and hear parts of the body while the patient was still alive.

**Antique Microscope**

In 1816, French doctor Rene Laennec invented the **stethoscope**. The stethoscope is a tool that allows doctors to hear a patient's heart, lungs, or other sounds inside the body. One day, Laennec noticed two children sending signals to each other. One child scratched the end of a long piece of wood with a pin. The other child put her ear to the other end of the wood to hear the scratching.

**Stethoscope**

Laennec thought the same idea might help him bring the sound of a patient's heart closer to his ear. He made a hollow tube of wood. He put one end on his patient's chest. Then he put the other end to his ear. Thump! Thump! Now doctors could gather information about the heart and lungs.

Before the thermometer, doctors touched a patient with their hand to decide if they had a fever. This method was not very accurate. So doctors tried to use a thermometer, which measured the air temperature, to measure a patient's body temperature. Early medical thermometers were very large and difficult to use. Recording a patient's temperature took 20 minutes!

**Modern Thermometers**

**Early Thermometer**

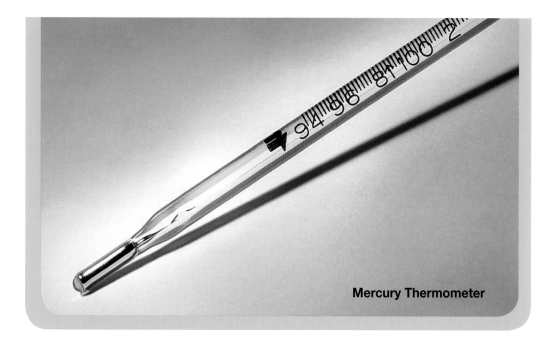

**Mercury Thermometer**

In 1866, English doctor Thomas Clifford Allbutt improved the medical thermometer. He made it six inches long (15.2 cm) and easy to carry. He also made it faster. His thermometer could record a patient's temperature in only five minutes. Soon, thermometers became part of every doctor's routine exam.

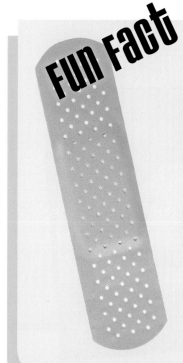

**Fun Fact**

Do you ever wonder who invented the Band-Aid? Earle Dickson was a cotton buyer for a company called Johnson & Johnson. His wife kept cutting her fingers when she cooked. Each time, she had to cut adhesive tape and gauze to cover the cut. The tape quickly lost its stick and the gauze fell off. Dickson wanted to create something for his wife that she could wear while her busy fingers kept moving. He designed a smaller gauze pad that was already attached to a piece of tape. He covered the tape with cloth to keep the gauze clean. Dickson's boss liked the idea so much the company decided to mass-produce it. The Band-Aid was born!

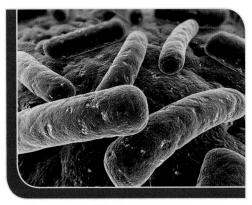
**Close-up of Bacteria**

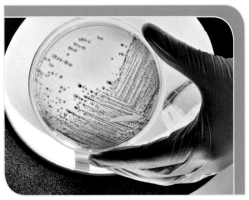
**E-coli Bacteria Growing in Lab Dish**

In the mid-1800s, many people died from infections in wounds or after surgery. Doctors thought that air caused the infections. English doctor Joseph Lister suspected something else might be causing the deadly infections. In 1865, he heard about Louis Pasteur and the idea that **microorganisms**, or tiny germs, might cause infection. To kill germs that he could not see, Lister used a carbolic acid solution to clean his patients' wounds. The solution was one of the first **antiseptics**.

Joseph Lister discovered that when he cleaned wounds with an antiseptic, patients were more likely to live.

**Did You Know?**
Antiseptics prevent infection by killing germs.

By the time Lister retired in 1883, most doctors were using his method of cleaning wounds. They also used steam to clean surgical instruments. Infection rates dropped and more patients lived.

**Surgical Instruments Being Cleaned**

# CHAPTER TWO

# Diagnosing Disease

In order to make patients feel better, doctors need to discover what is wrong with them. Doctors use different types of medical technology to see inside the body and diagnose disease.

Scientists study tissue samples under a microscope.

Microscopes are an important part of diagnosing disease. A microscope magnifies objects that are too small for the human eye to see. Some microscopes, called electron microscopes, can magnify cells thousands of times. Doctors use microscopes to examine samples from a patient's tissues or blood. For example, microscopes help doctors see tiny bacteria that cause infection. Microscopes can also show cancer cells growing in a tissue sample.

Microscope

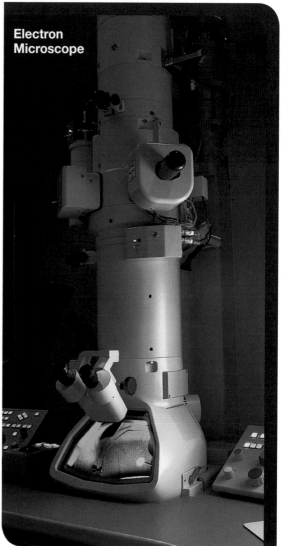

Electron Microscope

Viewing X-Ray

If you think you may have broken a bone, an x-ray is the quickest way to find out. X-rays are waves of electromagnetic energy. They travel in streams of tiny light **particles** called photons. When you have an x-ray taken a technician places an x-ray sensitive film on one side of your body. A machine shoots x-rays through you. The x-rays pass through soft tissue like skin and muscles. Harder parts like bones and teeth absorb more x-rays. Their shadows appear on the x-ray film.

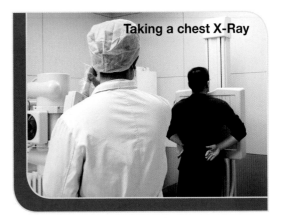
Taking a chest X-Ray

German physicist Wilhelm Roentgen first discovered x-rays by accident in 1895. While experimenting with electron beams and vacuum tubes he noticed that a screen in his lab was glowing. He held up different objects between the tube and the screen. When he put his hand in front of the tube Roentgen saw the shadow of his bones appear on the screen.

A CT or CAT scanner uses x-rays and computers to make images of the body. A CT scanner can see tissues inside solid organs like the heart or liver. A CT scanner is a big machine with a tunnel in the middle. The patient lies on a table that slides into the tunnel. Unlike an X-ray machine that sends only one beam of light, a CT scanner sends many narrow beams through a patient's body. A computer takes the pictures and builds a 3-D image.

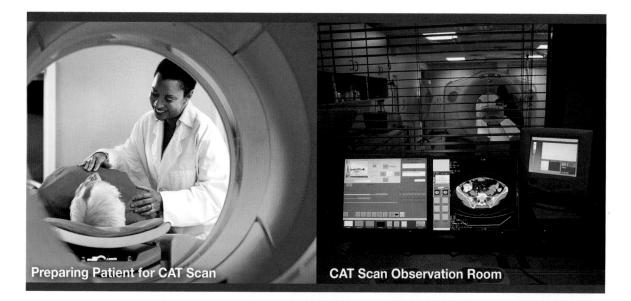

Preparing Patient for CAT Scan

CAT Scan Observation Room

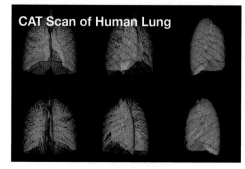

CAT Scan of Human Lung

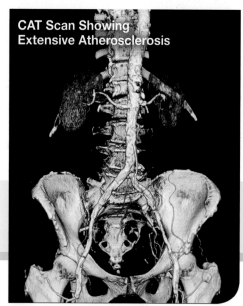

CAT Scan Showing Extensive Atherosclerosis

Doctors use the 3-D image to diagnose many diseases like cancer tumors and heart disease.

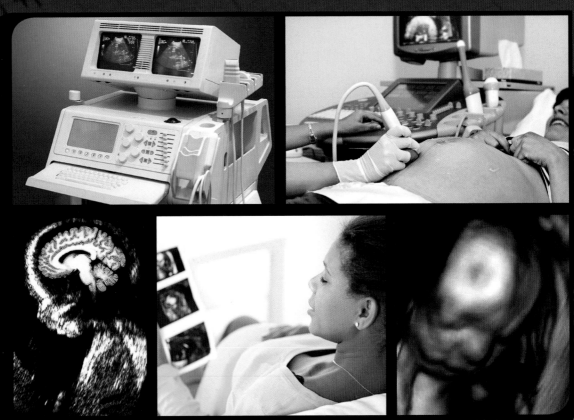

An ultrasound can help doctors find out the gender of an unborn baby and see if it is growing.

Ultrasound machines use sound waves that are too high for the human ear to hear. Ultrasound waves pass through the body and bounce back when they hit a solid surface. A receiver picks up each wave as it bounces back. A computer creates an image of an object's shape and location.

Magnetic resonance imaging (MRI) scans give a detailed picture of the soft tissues inside the body. An MRI uses magnetic fields to create images. MRIs allow doctors to more quickly diagnose and treat injuries. Many injured athletes have an MRI scan to diagnose a sprained knee or torn ligament.

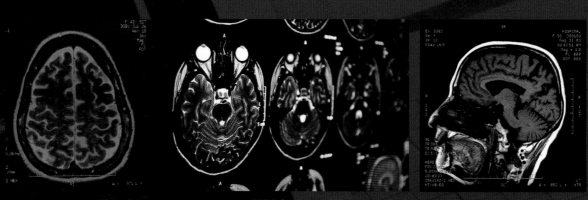

**MRI Scans of Brain**

**Preparing for MRI Scan**

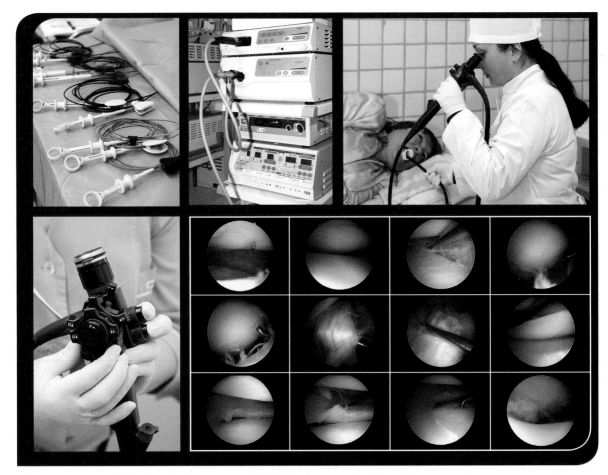

**Doctors use a lighted endoscope to see inside the esophagus and stomach.**

Endoscopes are tiny cameras that doctors place inside the body. They can see the inside of an organ. They can also take small tissue samples and remove foreign objects.

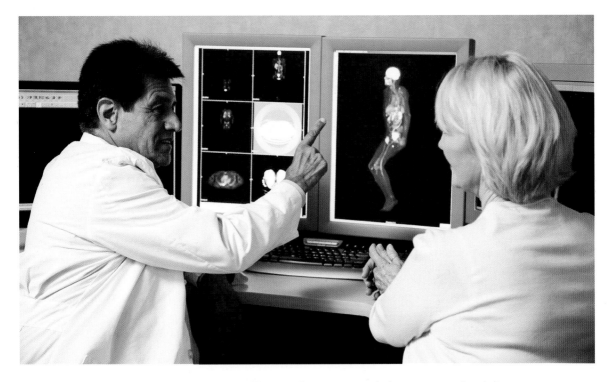

PET imaging uses **radioactive** materials to see inside the body. The radioactive material is **injected** into the body, swallowed, or inhaled. It builds up in the organ or area of the body being imaged. A special camera detects **emissions** from the radioactive material. It then builds a picture of the area.

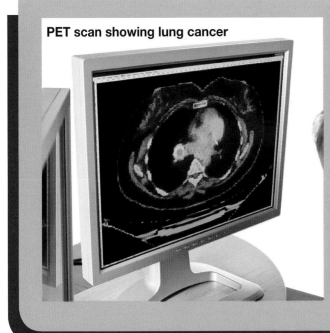

**PET scan showing lung cancer**

PET scans can measure important body functions such as blood flow and oxygen use. This information helps doctors determine how well a patient's organs and tissues are working. It is also used to find tiny cancer cells and see inside the brain.

# CHAPTER THREE

# medicine

Medicine can help sick people feel better. Sometimes medicine treats symptoms like fever or a sore throat. Some medicines can cure an illness. Other medicines can help prevent disease.

Many years ago, there was no **aspirin** or other painkillers. Instead, doctors brewed a tea from willow tree bark to ease pain. They discovered that something in the bark, called salicylic acid, eased pain. Chemist Felix Hoffman mixed it with another acid and created a new medicine called aspirin. Hoffman's father suffered from painful arthritis. Hoffman hoped his new medicine would help his father feel more comfortable.

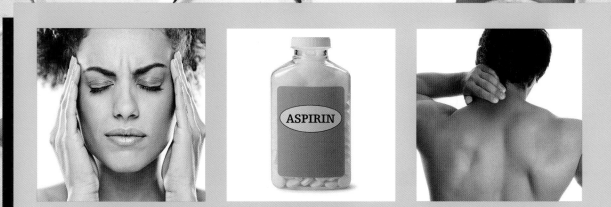

Since Hoffman's discovery, adults have been using aspirin for headaches and muscle pain. Most aspirin is in the form of pills. Doctors are learning that aspirin can be more than a pain reliever. It can be used to help prevent heart attacks and treat strokes.

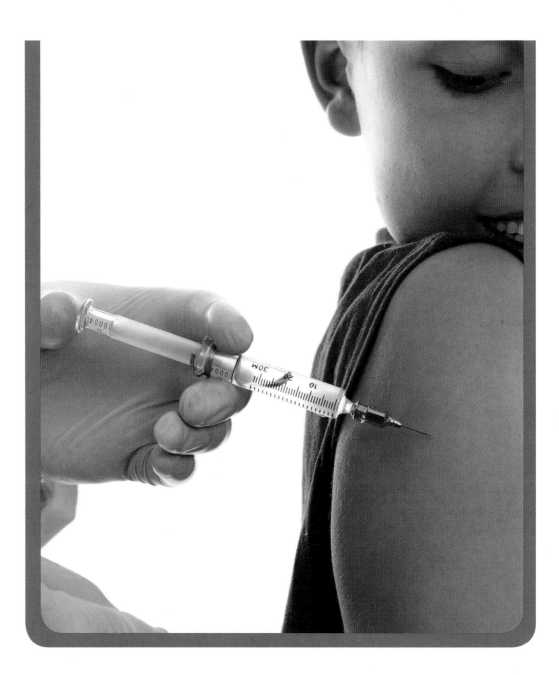

While some medicine can be swallowed as a pill, other medicine works better if it is injected directly into the body. Shots or injections use a **syringe** to deliver fluids directly into the blood or muscles. If you've had a shot, you've seen a syringe in action!

Before syringes, doctors used needles to put medicine into a patient's body. Because the needle was not sharp enough to pierce skin, doctors used it to put medicine through a natural body opening. Other times, they cut open a patient's skin to get the needle inside the body.

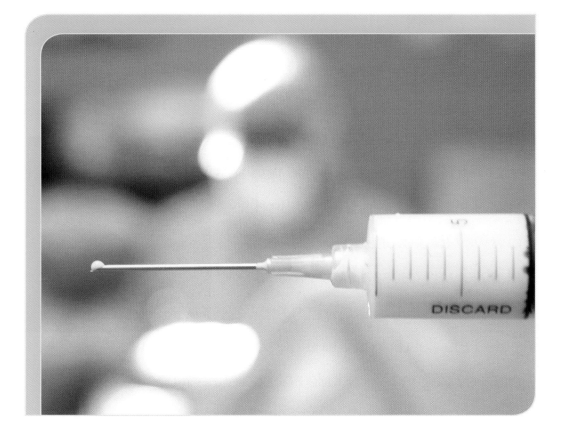

*Charles Gabriel Pravaz and Alexander Wood wanted to find a way to deliver medicine quickly. In 1883, they created a thin, hollow needle that was sharp enough to pierce the skin. The syringe could push the medicine into the body. The syringe could also pull out blood to be tested.*

Medicines called **vaccines** help prevent disease. In the 1950s, one in every 5,000 children died from a disease called polio. Those that survived often had damage to their legs and could no longer walk. Dr. Jonas Salk wanted to find a way to prevent polio. He knew that polio was caused by a virus. Salk killed the virus in his lab. When he injected the dead virus into a person,

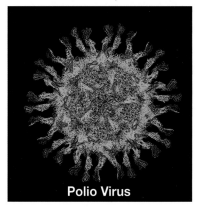

**Polio Virus**

their body began to produce antibodies. Antibodies fight a virus and protect a person against the disease. Since Salk's discovery of the polio vaccine, scientists have created vaccines for many other diseases.

Antibiotics are medicines used to treat infections caused by bacteria. An antibiotic works by either killing the bacteria or preventing it from multiplying. In 1928, English scientist Alexander Fleming discovered that a mold called penicillin appeared to kill bacteria in his lab. Several years later, scientists Howard Florey and Ernst Chain read about Fleming's findings. They believed that penicillin could save lives and make it easier to fight infections. In 1941, the men convinced the United States to mass-produce the medicine for its soldiers in World War II.

**Mold Growing on Bread**

**Closeup of Mold Growing on Bread**

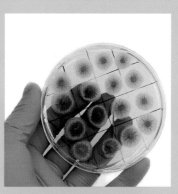

**Mold Growing in Petri Dish**

**Fun Fact**

In 1945, Florey, Chain, and Fleming each received the Nobel Prize for the development of the penicillin drug.

# CHAPTER FOUR
# surgery

During surgery, doctors cut open a patient's body to fight disease or repair parts that are not working well. Advances in medical technology allow surgeons to perform more and more amazing operations.

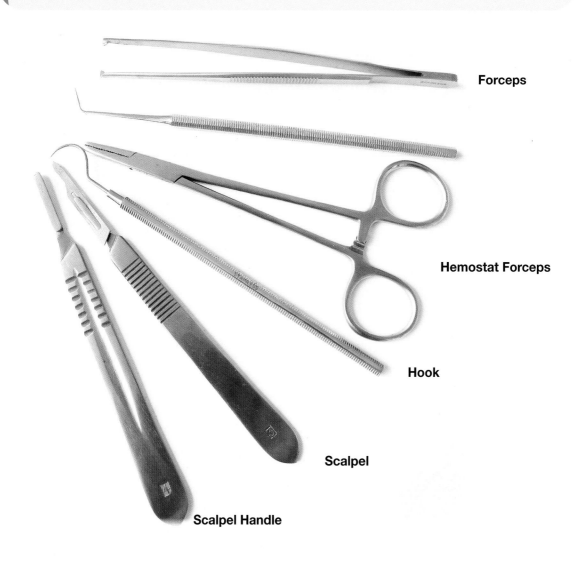

**Forceps**

**Hemostat Forceps**

**Hook**

**Scalpel**

**Scalpel Handle**

**Injectible Anesthesia**

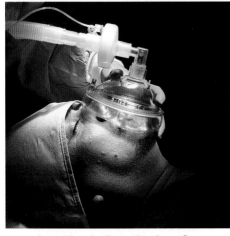

**Anesthesia Breathed as Gas**

**Local Anesthesia**

Doctors would not be able to perform complex surgeries without **anesthesia**. Anesthesia is medicine that makes sure a patient does not feel pain during surgery. Anesthesia can be injected into the blood or inhaled as a gas through a mask. Anesthesia can be local, like when a dentist numbs your gums and teeth before drilling a tooth. For major surgery, general anesthesia makes a patient fall into a deep sleep.

OUCH!

Before anesthesia, doctors had no way to help patients not feel pain. When surgery was needed to save a person's life, the patient was given a few swigs of an alcoholic drink. Surgeons had to work quickly while assistants held the patient down.

Before the heart-lung bypass machine, heart surgery was very risky. Surgeons tried to operate on the heart while it was still beating. With the heart-lung machine, surgeons can stop a patient's heart for several hours during surgery. The machine takes over the heart's job. It circulates the patient's blood and removes carbon dioxide waste gas. It pumps the patient's blood through an artificial lung where it receives oxygen. It then pumps the blood back into the patient's body.

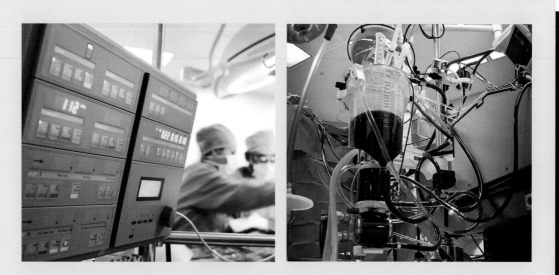

Using the heart-lung machine, many new operations are possible. Surgeons can repair congenital heart defects. They can replace damaged heart valves. They can also perform bypass surgery to replace blocked arteries.

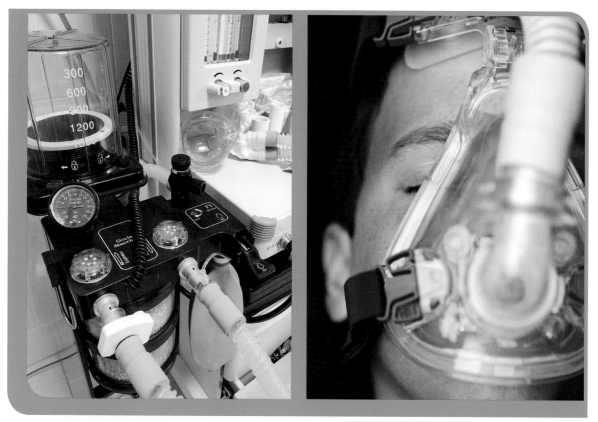

**Ventilator**                    **Ventilator mask**

A ventilator is a machine that helps a patient breathe. Ventilators get oxygen into the lungs and remove carbon dioxide gas from the body. These machines are often used during surgery when a patient is under general anesthesia. The ventilator makes sure the patient keeps breathing during surgery. Sometimes ventilators are used for people who have long-term breathing problems.

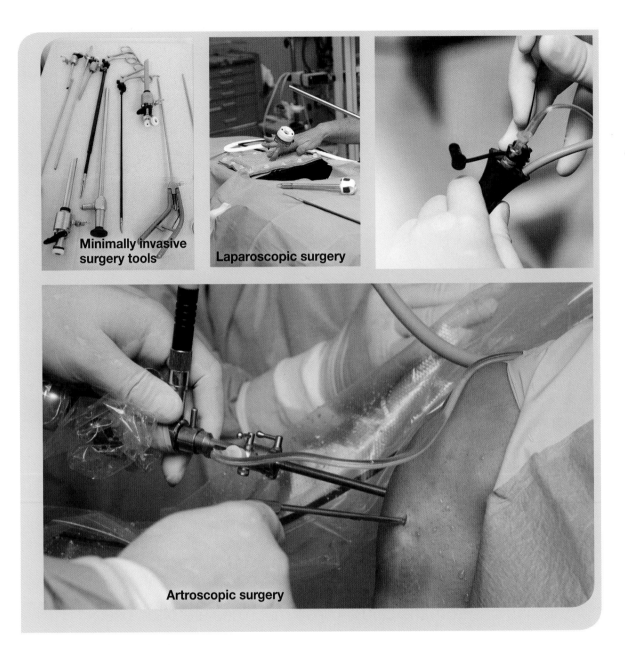

Minimally invasive surgery tools

Laparoscopic surgery

Artroscopic surgery

Laparoscopic surgery allows doctors to perform operations without making a large cut in a patient's body. Instead, the surgeon makes a tiny cut in the patient's belly button. The surgeon inserts a tube with a tiny camera through the cut. A few other small cuts are made for instruments the surgeon will need during the operation.

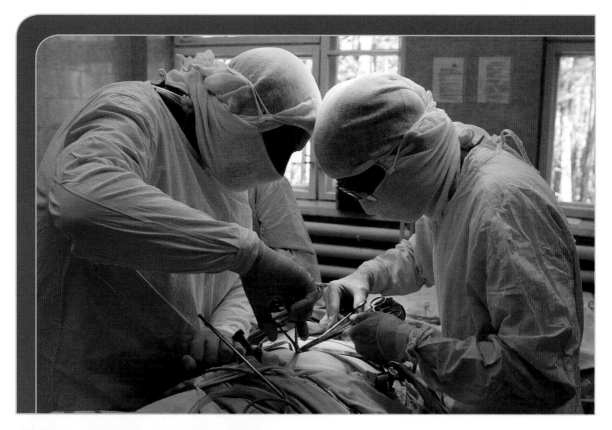

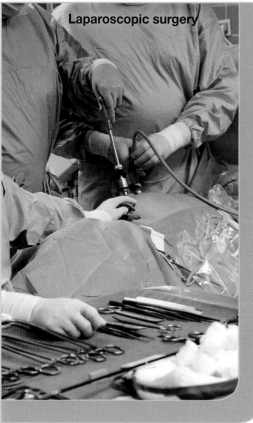

Laparoscopic surgery

Surgeons and patients prefer laparoscopic surgery. The incisions are smaller which means patients heal faster and have less scarring. Patients can also leave the hospital sooner. They report having less pain after laparoscopic surgery.

During the surgery, the camera projects images from inside the body onto a video screen in the operating room. The surgeon watches the screen and controls the instruments from outside the body. Because there are no large cuts, most patients heal quickly after laparoscopic surgery.

In some cases, surgeons use robots to perform surgery. Using robots allows surgeons to have greater control of surgical instruments. Robotic arms do not have the tiny tremors that a human hand can make. This allows surgeons to perform operations that are more intricate.

The success of robotic surgery depends largely on the surgeon's skill with handling the robotics.

When using a robot, surgeons insert instruments and cameras through small cuts in a patient's body. The surgeon sits at a console next to the patient. He looks through a viewfinder at a 3-D image sent by the camera. The surgeon works the robot's surgical arms using hand and foot controls.

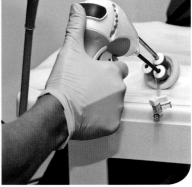

Doctors can also use lasers for surgery. Lasers are powerful beams of light that can be focused on a tiny area. In laser surgery, the surgeon cuts tissue with the laser instead of a scalpel.

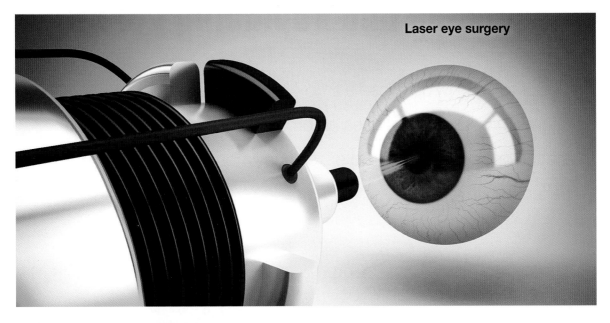

**Laser eye surgery**

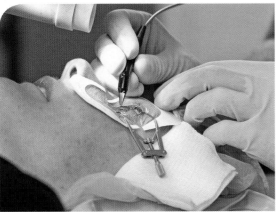

Lasers do many things. They operate on the eye. They remove scars and birthmarks. Lasers can also be used to seal blood vessels in surgery and unclog arteries. Lasers can also help destroy cancerous tumors and cells.

Millions of people who no longer need glasses can thank Dr. Stephen Trokel. Dr. Trokel developed laser eye surgery to improve a patient's vision. He performed the first laser eye surgery in 1987. Since then, millions of laser eye surgeries have been performed, helping people see better all over the world.

# rebuilding and replacing parts

Sometimes people lose a limb or organ in an accident. Other times, disease causes an organ not to function. Medical technology can help rebuild or replace limbs and organs for patients.

Athlete with a right below knee prosthetic running leg.

If an organ no longer works properly, doctors can replace it with an **organ transplant**. Most of the time, organ donors are people who have died but wanted to donate their healthy organs to help others. Sometimes, living donors can donate a kidney or a piece of liver to a patient. Surgeons remove the old organ and attach the donated organ in its place. There is a risk that a patient's body will reject the new organ. His or her immune system may attack it and try to destroy it. To prevent organ rejection, transplant patients take anti-rejection medicine for the rest of their lives.

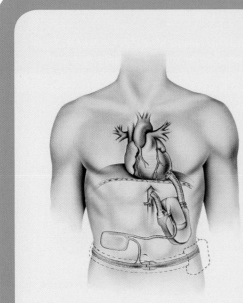

Artificial hearts can help some patients stay alive while they wait for a donor for a heart transplant. The artificial heart pumps blood through the body. In 1982, Barney Clark received the first artificial heart. He lived for 112 days after surgery. Today, most patients who receive artificial hearts live about five months longer.

If a person is missing an arm or leg, a doctor can replace it with an artificial one. An artificial limb is also called a **prosthesis**. A prosthesis can look very similar to a real limb.

Actor Owen Wilson visits the Naval Medical Center in San Diego to meet an injured soldier with a myoelectric arm.

A myoelectric arm is one type of artificial arm. Whenever a muscle in the body contracts, it causes a chemical reaction that sends a small electrical signal called an "EMG". **Electrodes** that are attached to the surface of the skin record the signal and amplify it. The signal travels to a controller that switches small electric motors in the arm, hand, or wrist on or off. This moves the arm.

**Electrodes**

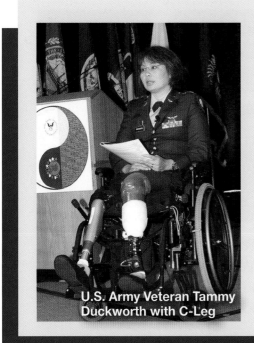

U.S. Army Veteran Tammy Duckworth with C-Leg

C-legs are artificial legs that use a **microprocessor** to help people walk. The C-leg has computerized sensors record the 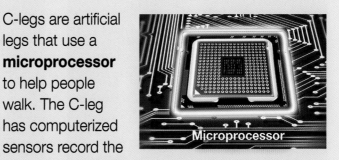 strain applied to the knee and leg. The sensors send these readings to a microprocessor 50 times a second. The microprocessor then makes quick adjustments so that the artificial leg can match the patient's walking speed.

Microprocessor

Artificial or bionic eyes may one day return sight to people. Millions of people are affected by diseases that damage the eye's **retina**. These diseases often lead to blindness.

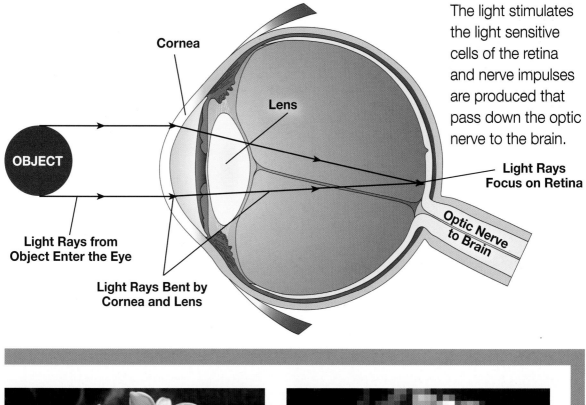

Cornea

Lens

Light Rays from Object Enter the Eye

Light Rays Bent by Cornea and Lens

OBJECT

The light stimulates the light sensitive cells of the retina and nerve impulses are produced that pass down the optic nerve to the brain.

Light Rays Focus on Retina

Optic Nerve to Brain

Normal Vision

Bionic Eye Simulated Vision

Scientists are working on an electronic device to replace the retina. In 2011, German researchers created an artificial retina. Their bionic eye has sensors that detect light. It turns light into a pattern of electrical impulses. Currently, the bionic eye does not see in color. It also is much less detailed than normal vision.

Medical technology can also help people hear.
A cochlear implant is a small electronic device that helps
a person hear sound.

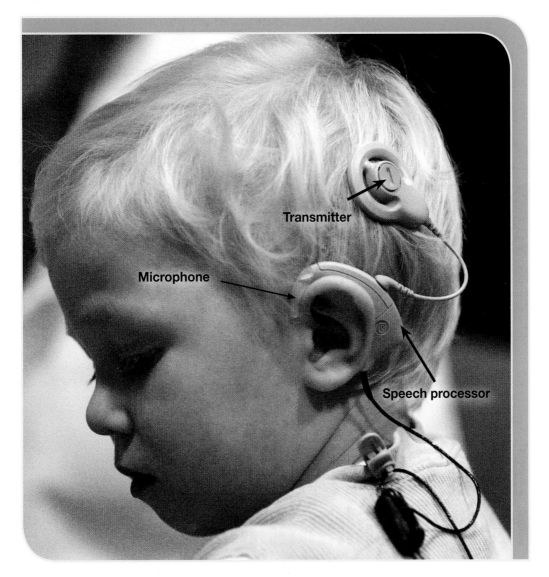

Transmitter

Microphone

Speech processor

A microphone picks up sounds from the environment. It sends the sounds to a speech processor that selects and arranges the sounds. The sounds travel through a transmitter to a receiver. The receiver converts the sounds into electrical impulses. Electrodes collect the impulses and send them to the different parts of the auditory nerve. The nerve passes the signals to the brain. The brain recognizes the signals as sound.

# the future of medical technology

In the future, new medical technologies will be possible. Every day, scientists research innovative technology. Their discoveries may help people live longer and healthier lives.

Doctors may look at a patient's **genes** to diagnose a disease. Every cell inside your body has genes. Genes hold the instructions that decide what you look like and how your body works. Each person has different genes. Scientists have learned that some genes are related to different diseases. For example, some genes give a person a higher risk of developing heart disease or cancer. Scientists have also found that genes can affect how medicines work for a person. They may use genes to decide what treatment or medicine to prescribe.

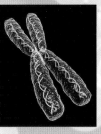

# Human Genome Project

In 1990, many scientists started a project to map out all the genes in the human body. The Human Genome Project found more than 1,800 disease related genes.

Some diseases like cystic fibrosis are caused by defective genes. Scientists are studying genetic therapy as a way to treat or prevent these diseases. Using genetic therapy, scientists insert healthy genes into

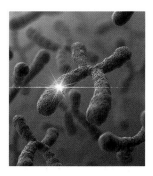

a patient's cells. The healthy genes replace the ones that are not working properly. Scientists are experimenting with ways to deliver the healthy genes. Some are using special viruses that carry the healthy genes inside the patient's cells. Scientists hope that someday genetic therapy will cure diseases caused by genes.

DNA test sequence

Culture flask

Your body has millions of cells. Cells specialize depending on their function. Your cells become heart cells, blood cells, and brain cells. A stem cell is a cell that has not yet specialized. It has the potential to become any type of cell.

Stem cells may one day allow doctors to grow new organs or tissues. Stem cells may also be used to treat diseases like diabetes and cancer.

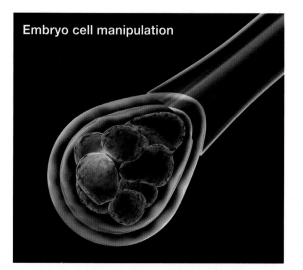
Embryo cell manipulation

In 2007, English veterinarians removed stem cells from a racehorse. They purified and multiplied the cells in the lab. A few weeks later, they injected the stem cells back into the horse's tendon. The stem cells grew into new tissue that repaired damage in the horse's limb.

Stem cells are found in different tissues in the body. They are also found in human embryos. Some people have a moral objection to stem cell research that uses embryos. Scientists are researching how stem cells may treat many serious diseases such as diabetes and cancer. They believe that stem cells hold great promise for treating many incurable diseases.

**43**

Scientists hope nanotechnology will improve medical technology in the future. Nanotechnology is working with materials at the nanoscale level. A nanometer is one billionth of a meter. To compare, one human hair is about 80,000 nanometers wide.

Nanotechnology would work with the smallest parts of the body such as cells, molecules, and atoms. Tiny nanobot robots could be programmed to perform functions in and out of the body. They could repair damage to tiny cells. Nano devices could be placed in the body to prevent disease and repair damage before it becomes a serious problem.

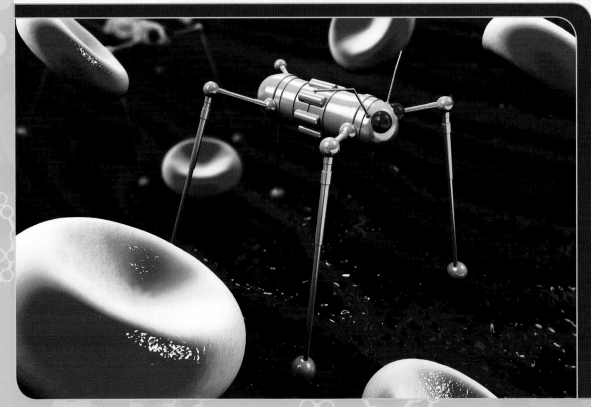

**Nano-sized drugs could be made to seek out the site of a disease and deliver the medicine directly to the right part of the body, without damaging tissue around it.**

Medical technology has helped people live healthier and longer lives. Every day, new discoveries improve how doctors treat patients. The latest advances are bringing people with different skills together. Doctors, scientists, computer programmers, and engineers are working together to make our lives healthier.

# Glossary

**anesthesia** (an-uhs-THEE-zhuh): medicine or gas given to people before an operation to prevent them from feeling pain

**antibiotics** (an-it-bye-OT-ikz): medicines that kill bacteria and are used to cure infections and diseases

**antiseptics** (an-ti-SEP-tikss): substances that kill germs and prevent infection by stopping the growth of germs

**aspirin** (ASS-pi-rin): a medicine that relieves pain and reduces fever

**diagnose** (dye-uhg-NOHSS): to determine what disease a patient has or what is causing their problem

**electrodes** (i-LEK-trodes): points through which an electric current can flow into or out of a device or substance

**emissions** (i-MISH-uhnz): substances released into the air

**genes** (JEENZ): one of the parts of the cells of all living things that determine how you look and the way you grow

**injected** (in-JEKT-ed): used a needle and syringe to put medicine into someone's body

**microorganisms** (mye-kroh-OR-guh-niz-uhmz): living things that are too small to be seen without a microscope

**microprocessor** (MAHY-kroh-pros-es-er): a computer circuit

**organ transplant** (OR-guhn TRANSS-plant): a surgical operation in which a diseased organ is replaced by a healthy organ

**particles** (PAR-tuh-kuhlz): extremely small pieces of something

**prosthesis** (pross-THEE-siss): an artificial device that replaces a missing part of a body

**radioactive** (ray-dee-oh-AK-tiv): materials that are made up of atoms whose nuclei break down, giving off radiation

**retina** (RET-uhn-uh): the lining at the back of the eyeball that sends images of the things you see to the brain

**stethoscope** (STETH-uh-skope): an instrument used to listen to the sounds from a patient's heart, lungs, and other areas

**syringe** (suh-RINJ): a tube with a plunger and a hollow needle used to give injections

**vaccines** (vac-SEENZ): a medicine that causes a person to produce antibodies that protect him or her from a disease

# Index

## Websites to Visit

www.nlm.nih.gov/hmd/especiallyfor/teachersstudents.html

www.sciencenewsforkids.org/pages/about.asp

www.scrubclub.org/home.aspx

## About the Author

Carla Mooney has always been fascinated by medicine and the latest breakthroughs in medical technology. She has a Bachelor of Science degree from the University of Pennsylvania and has written more than 25 books for young people. Today, she lives with her husband and three children near Pittsburgh, Pennsylvania.

**Meet The Author!**
www.meetREMauthors.com